JOKES & RIDDLES

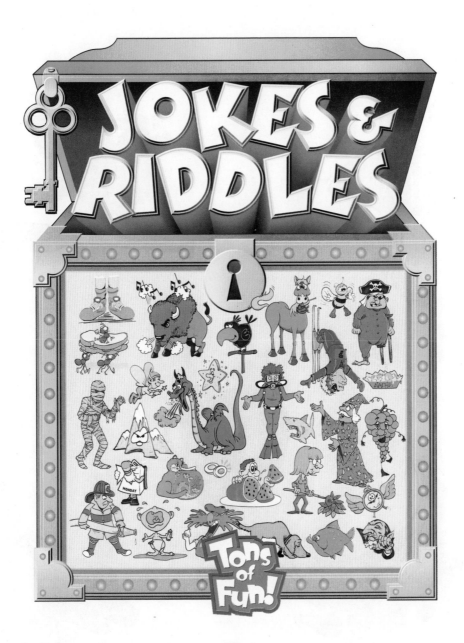

By
Chris Tait

kidsbooks

Visit us at **www.kidsbooks.com**

INTRODUCTION

What's funnier than a chicken crossing the road? How about a skateboarding dog? Turn the page for the most hilarious jokes and riddles around. There are tons of knock-knock knee slappers, silly school jokes, awesome animal jokes, and much, much more. So what are you waiting for? Get ready for some side-splitting laughter with your friends and family!

KNOCK, KNOCK!

Knock, knock!
Who's there?
Homer!
Homer who?
Homer again after a long day of school. Time to have some fun!

Knock, knock!
Who's there?
Jason!
Jason who?
Jason your brother around the house will get you in trouble!

Knock, knock!
Who's there?
Wah Zeen!
Wah Zeen who?
Wah Zeen me who broke your window, honest!

Knock, knock!
Who's there?
Howell!
Howell who?
Howell I ever get in if you don't open the door?

Knock, knock!
Who's there?
Daisy!
Daisy who?
Daisy goes to school, nights he plays baseball!

Knock, knock!
Who's there?
Polly!
Polly who?
Polly wogs are just baby frogs!

Knock, knock!
Who's there?
Diane!
Diane who?
Diane to play football, let's go!

Knock, knock!
Who's there?
Jerry!
Jerry who?
Jerry funny. You know
who it is!

Knock, knock!
Who's there?
Peter!
Peter who?
Peter me! You're just going to have to
decide, once and for all, which of us
it's going to be!

Knock, knock!
Who's there?
Pucker!
Pucker who?
Pucker up, I'm gonna kiss you!

Knock, knock!
Who's there!
Dana!
Dana who?
Dana talk to me like that!

Knock, knock!
Who's there?
Alfred!
Alfred who?
Alfred I got the wrong door.
Sorry!

SILLY SPIES

What did they call the double agent who was always calling home?

A phone-y!

What do you call a spy who ends up in jail?

Con-fidential!

Why was the spy looking in the want ads?

Because the information she needed was classified!

What code name did they give to the spy who chewed gum?

Bubble-oh-seven!

What did the secret agent say when he had tracked down the lost goalie?

"Finders keepers!"

What did the secret agent say when she was looking for the missing livestock?

"Ollie, ollie, oxen free!"

What do spies put at the top of every memo?

Re: search!

What did the spy say when he left his papers in his filing cabinet?

"I'll have to check with the Bureau on that one!"

What do rude spies use to communicate?

Coarse code!

What do you call a spy with bad posture?

A stooped snoop!

What did the computer spy get from the Internet virus?

A hacking cough!

What did the secret agent say when he mistook a bison for a cow?

"Sorry, it was an ox-idant!"

Where did the detective find the missing porridge?

In the mush-room!

What did the spy say when he woke to find two Xs written on him?

"I've been double-crossed!"

Wacky Wizardry

What did the wizard say when he saw a bull in the sky?

"It must be a bull moon!"

When did the dragon finally get full?

Around mid-knight!

What do you call the wizard who is hungry for astronomy?

Star-ving!

What did the witch say for a spell to get jewelry?

"Boil and bauble!"

Where did the wizard keep the power source for his basement?

In the dungeon-erator!

What did the wizard call the statues on his walls when the sun made them hot?

Gar-boils!

Where did the wizard keep the seeds for his garden?

Up in the flower tower!

What did the wizard call the king of the monsters in Scotland?

His Loch Ness Highness!

What did the wizard say when he had to sell one of his paintings?

"It's only a poor-trait!"

How did the monster scare the wizard?

He crypt up on him!

Why did the wizard's butler wear a suit of armor?

Because he was a Sir-vant!

Where did the wizard go to withdraw a crystal ball?

To a fortune teller!

What did the wizard get when he crossed a skunk with a TV set?

Smell-o-vision!

What did the wizard say about the stupid monarch?

"He ruled the whole king-dumb!"

What did the wizard call the young royal who kept falling down?

Prince Harming!

What did the wizard call the king who wouldn't come down out of the tower?

His Royal High-ness!

XTREME-LY FUNNY

Why did the boy tell his father to go sit on the ski hill?

Because his mother wanted a cold pop!

 1

What was the surfer named Ace most afraid of?

Card sharks!

 2

What did the boarder say when he saw his sibling sticking partway out of the snow?

"Hey, look, it's my half-brother!"

3

What did the young surfer say about the old surfer who worked at the seafood restaurant?

"I can't believe she soled out!"

 4

What did the skier say about the snowboarding feline?

"Now that's one cool cat!"

What do you call the part of a wooden surfboard without holes?

Knot holes!

 5

Police officer: "I'll teach you to skate here, young man!"

Skater: "I wish you would. We keep wiping out!"

6

Knock, knock!
Who's there?
Island!
Island who?
Island perfectly
every time I skydive!

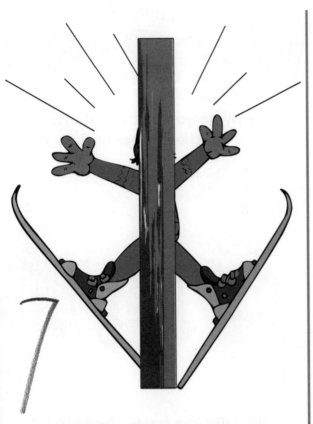

What did the skater say after skating behind a car for a few minutes?

"Man, I'm exhausted!"

What did the surfboard say to the termite?

"Stop boring me!"

Why did the diver fill his pockets with pencils?

He thought the lead would weigh him down!

Why did the surfer bail so big his first time on television?

Because he wanted to make a big splash!

How did the skier feel when he ran into the telephone pole?

He was shocked!

What did the shark say when it saw the surfers pull up in a Jeep?

"Look, canned food!"

What did the surfers say while they waited for the tide to come in?

"Long time, no sea!"

UNDER WHERE?

What do you call someone who wears camouflage boxers?

Under cover!

Knock, knock!
Who's there?
Izzy!
Izzy who?
Izzy wearing any underwear?

What do you call stockings that blow in the breeze?

Wind socks!

What did the designer think about her new line of hosiery?

She thought it was a big sock-sess!

What do you call a Scottish stocking puppet?

The Sock-Ness monster!

Why do you put wet shorts on the clothesline?

So they'll be high and dry!

Why did the boxer shorts like being on the clothesline?

They just started to get the hang of it!

Why didn't the boxer shorts want to be put away?

Because they thought it would hamper their style!

How did the dress feel about the see-through tights?

Sheer delight!

Why did the socks feel so confident?

Because they knew that they were a shoe-in!

What do you call all your favorite underwear when it's together for the first time?

A boxed set!

How quickly did the young man put on his boxers?

In a zip!

What kind of insect lives in some underwear?

The button fly!

What do you call the peg where you hang up your underwear?

The butt-on!

Knock, knock!
Who's there?
Butter!
Butter who?
Butter make sure your underwear isn't showing!

What is it called when someone works out in his underwear?

Boxer-cize!

SILLY SPIES

What do you call testimony that doesn't stand up in court?

Wilt-ness!

What do you ask a secret agent to do in court?

Testi-spy!

What do you pay a secret agent to speak in court?

Testi-money!

What did the secret agent call the bowling ball that she took to court?

Heavy-dence!

What did the spy say when he split his pants?

"Let me check my briefs!"

Where did the secret agent find the enemy chef?

In her hidden fork-tress!

How did the heavy spy escape?

He dug a ton-el!

What did the sign on the nuclear lab's door say when the spy arrived?

"Gone fission!"

Gone Fission

Where did the spy have to go to find the enemy spy's baker?

To his secret breadquarters!

What did the spy wearing shorts say to the secret agent?

"Meet me at the cutoffs!"

Why did the spy know to look for the enemy agent in the wild?

Because he was a cheat-ah!
(cheetah)

How did the spy know that his enemy would come out of her underground lair?

Because she always caved in!

What did the spy say when she caught someone snooping in her front yard?

"Stop in the name of the lawn!"

What did the detective say when he caught the cold-hearted killer?

"Freeze!"

Wacky Wizardry

What did the wizard get when he crossed a python with a drinking cup?

A snake in the glass!

What did the wizard call the cow that went over the moon?

High jumper!

What did the wizard call the horse's back?

A mane frame!

What kind of nuts do frogs like?

Croak-o-nuts!

Where did the country wizard go to get supplies?

The farm-acy!

How did the wizard feel when a satellite fell into his yard?

 Star struck!

When the young wizard turned a dog into a frog, what did his father say?

"What did I tell you about cursing in the house?"

WOOF!

What do wizards put in potions to make people gain weight?

In-greed-ients!

☆ ☽ ☆

What color was the wizard's cat?

Purr-ple!

☆ ☀ ☆

What do you call a wizard who loves telescopes?

Astrono-merlin!

☆ ☽ ☆

What did the wizard say about the rowboat going around the moat?

"Looks like it's in oar-bit!"

How did the star-happy wizard like to eat his cookies?

With a Milky Way!

☆ ☽ ☆

What did the astronomer wizard sing in the bath?

"When You Wash Upon a Star"!

☆ ☀ ☆

What did the wizard get when he stuck his nose in a jar?

Ring around the nosie!

☆ ☽ ☆

What dish do goblins like best?

Mon-stir fry!

☆ ☀ ☆

Why do wizards have stars and moons on their hats?

They need a little personal space!

KNOCK, KNOCK!

Knock, knock!
Who's there?
Sheepritty!
Sheepritty who?
Sheepritty, don't you think?

Knock, knock!
Who's there?
Deannie!
Deannie who?
Deannie hear me the first time?

Knock, knock!
Who's there?
Chuck!
Chuck who?
Chuck me the ball and quit asking so many questions!

Knock, knock!
Who's there?
Fishes!
Fishes who?
Fishes temper that dog's got. He should be on a leash!

Knock, knock!
Who's there?
Disguise!
Disguise who?
Disguise killing me with these knock-knock jokes!

Knock, knock!
Who's there?
Emma!
Emma who?
Emma bugging you yet?

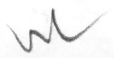

Knock, knock!
Who's there?
Chair!
Chair who?
Chair you go again, asking
silly questions!

Knock, knock!
Who's there?
Amy!
Amy who?
Amy 'fraid I may have the
wrong house! You don't look
familiar at all!

Knock, knock!
Who's there?
Discus!
Discus who?
Discus throwing inside will
get you detention!

Knock, knock!
Who's there?
Holly!
Holly who?
Holly cow, Boss, it's time to head
back to the hideout!

Knock, knock!
Who's there?
Doughnut!
Doughnut who?
Doughnut make me reveal my true
identity! I'm undercover!

Knock, knock!
Who's there?
Patty O.!
Patty O. who?
Patty O'Furniture!

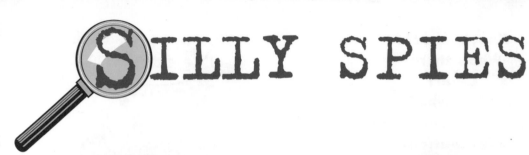

SILLY SPIES

Why was the spy so afraid of insects?

Because he knew that he was being bugged!

What did the spy say when she found out that her phone was being tapped?

"When will these guys stop bugging me?"

What did the doctor write in the spy's fitness report?

"This agent is in tip-tap shape!"

What do you call a spy who's a bug?

Insect-or Gadget!

Why did the spy go to work dressed as a bee?

Because she'd heard there was going to be a sting!

What did the spy do when he heard that he had to dig a tunnel?

He tried to worm his way out of it!

What did the detective say to the chicken?

"I have to appre-hen-d you!"

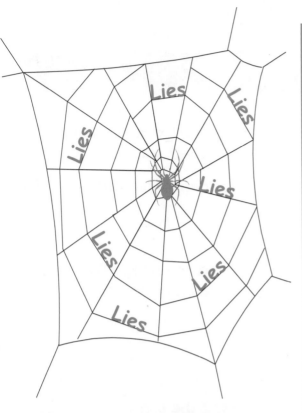

Why did the spy nickname her enemy "The Spider"?

Because he lived in a web of lies!

What did the spy say to the bee?

"Buzz off!"

What did the spy have to take after being bitten by a bug?

Ant-ibiotics!

Why did the detective think that the spy had wings?

Because he was a fly-by-night!

How did the spy get to the honey?

She followed the bee-trail! (betrayal)

What do you call a wire-tapping rabbit spy?

Bugs bunny!

What kind of critters do secret agents like?

Spy-ders!

XTREME-LY FUNNY

How does it feel to sit in front of a fire after skiing all day?

Grate!

Why did the motocrosser ride his bike?

Because it was too heavy to carry!

What was the highest mountain before Mt. Everest was discovered?

Mt. Everest!

Knock, knock!
Who's there?
Olaf!
Olaf who?
Olaf my skis at the bottom of the hill!

What did the young surfer say to the old surfer, who could remember when a phone call cost 10 cents?

"Hey, dimes have changed!"

Why don't boarders ever wear watches?

Because they know that time flies!

Why did the hang glider put his watch on the ground?

He wanted to fly over time!

Why did the climber take her watch up the mountain with her?

She wanted to see time travel!

Why did the skateboarder take a pumpkin off the jump with him?

Because he wanted to make squash!

What did the dirty biker say when it started to rain really hard?

"If this keeps up, my name will be mud!"

What did the tired mountain biker say after crashing into the shrubs?

"Man, am I bushed!"

Did you hear the story about the skateboarder who snapped the back of her board?

It's a sad tail!

Why did the surfer wipe out?

Because he was blinded by the sunfish!

Why was the surfer so happy to swim with dolphins?

Because she felt that she really had a porpoise!

No Wacky Wizardry

Why did the wizard say that you should
never warm up to a snake?

Because they're cold-blooded!

What did the wizard call his hallways
after he had
snakeskin wallpaper installed?

His rept-aisles!

What animal does the wizard
say is always lying?

The bull-frog!

What did the wizard call his
favorite reptile?

The Lizard of Oz!

What is the wizard's favorite
swamp flower?

The croak-us!

What did the frog say to his son who
was late for school?

"Hop to it!"

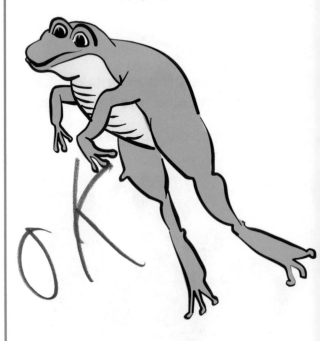

What did the wizard use to warn other drivers that he was coming?

A frog-horn!

What did the wizard's son say when the wizard started to tell him the reptile joke?

"You already toad me that one!"

What did the wizard call his smallest fishing rod?

A tad-pole!

What did the cat in the wizard's castle have to do?

Mousework!

How do frogs get clean?

They use croak-on-a-rope!

What do you call the wizard who collects wildlife from the swamp?

A toad-hog!

Where did the wizard go to turn the student back into a boy?

The changing room!

What did the wizard say when his cat caught a mouse?

"Micely done!"

What did the wizard's blackbird think about the big party?

Oh, he was raven about it!

Was the wizard's blackbird hungry after the party?

He was raven-ous!

COMIC CRITTERS

What are the first notes of the monkeys' 5th Symphony?

Ba-na-na-na!

What kind of animal has the best color in summer?

The orangu-tan!

What do you call a seat for a frog?

A toad-stool!

What is the coolest animal in the swamp?

The hip-o!

What do you call a sleeping lizard?

A calm-eleon!

How do you know that you've seen a leopard?

Oh, they're easy to spot!

What do you see when a bear has its head in a blueberry bush?

Its bear bottom!

Who can you use to make calls
in a swamp?

A croc-o-dial!

What birds are twice as fun
as the rest?

*The cock-a-two and the
pair-a-keet!*

Where do you put your
jumping friends from Australia?

In the kanga-room!

What animal is no fun at a party?

The boar!

 SILLY SPIES

Why did the secret agent look for clues in a pasture?

Because he wanted to do his first field assignment!

What happened to the sketch artist?

He disappeared without a trace!

What did the detective say to the dessert?

"I have to put you in protective custard-y!"

What do secret agents do for fun?

Play catch!

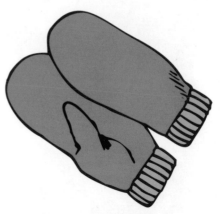

Why did Soviet spies always wear mittens?

Because they were in the Cold War!

What did the silly sleuth say to the conductor?

"I have to de-train you for questioning!"

Why do spies love the snow?

Because it's a hint-er wonderland!

Why was the spy worried about his socks while spying on the golfers?

Because he had a hole in one!

cough cough

What did the sick secret agent say to the criminal?

"Hold out your hands so I can cough (cuff) you!"

What did the secret agent say to the Riddler?

"I have to take you in for questioning!"

Why did the spy follow her enemy to the races?

Because she wanted to track him down!

Why was the spy hiding in the butcher shop?

Because she thought that was where the steak-out was!

What do you call it when a secret agent comes out of hiding?

Dis-cover!

Why was the spy afraid of airplanes?

She was afraid that someone would identi-fly her!

EXTREME-LY FUNNY

What did the boarder say when she slipped on a banana skin?

"I didn't find that very a-peeling!"

What did the towrope say to the boarder?

"Hey, can I give you a lift?"

Why is the most famous signature board like Lassie?

Because it's a star with a tail!

Why are dogs such bad skaters?

Because they have two left feet— and two right ones!

What game do boarders play when they're bored?

Ride and seek!

Why did the BMXer love his hilarious doctor?

Because she kept him in stitches!

Why is it hard to play cards on a windsurfer?

Because you have to stand on the deck!

Why did the climber think that she was going to be in a movie after her accident?

Because she had to be in the cast right away!

How do lost surfers clean their clothes?

They wash ashore!

How did the biker feel after biking
across the archery practice range?

*As if he had made
an arrow escape!*

Why did the climber in the cast feel
like an old record?

He was all scratchy!

What did the boarder say to his
friend William, who was in his way?

Will, you get out of my way!

What did the chilly boarders sing
on New Year's Eve?

"Freeze a jolly good fellow!"

Knock, knock!
Who's there?
Snow!
Snow who?
*Snow way I'm going
rock climbing—it's too dangerous!*

Why did the diver begin her dive
in shallow water?

*Because she wanted to start
on a small scale!*

Why did the skater put her board
in the freezer?

*Because she wanted to
chill out her style!*

KNOCK, KNOCK!

Knock, knock!
Who's there?
Albany!
Albany who?
Albany of these knock-knock jokes are there, anyway?

Knock, knock!
Who's there?
Ray!
Ray who?
Ray-member the last time I was here?

Knock, knock!
Who's there?
Tommy!
Tommy who?
Tommy you'll always be special!

Knock, knock!
Who's there?
Glenda!
Glenda who?
Glenda hand, man, this is heavy!

Knock, knock!
Who's there?
Dougie!
Dougie who?
Dougie hole in your lawn by accident! Sorry!

Knock, knock!
Who's there?
Isabel!
Isabel who?
Isabel out of order? I had to knock!

Knock, knock!
Who's there?
Seek!
Seek who?
Seek-rat agent. That's a seek-rat I can't tell!

Knock, knock!
Who's there?
Alfred!
Alfred who?
Alfred the needle if you'll tie the knot!

Knock, knock!
Who's there?
Gadget!
Gadget who?
Gadget in your glove or it'll hit you in the head!

Knock, knock!
Who's there?
Arizona!
Arizona who?
Arizona so many times I can knock!

Knock, knock!
Who's there?
A. Pierre!
A. Pierre who?
A. Pierre at five o'clock, and you'll find out!

Knock, knock!
Who's there?
Adolph!
Adolph who?
Adolph ball hit me in de mowf!

Wacky Wizardry

Why couldn't the cat talk after catching the rodent?

It had a mouse-ful!

Why did the wizard's cat want to put rodents in the freezer?

It wanted to make mice cubes!

What did the wizard get when he crossed his hamster with a bodybuilder?

A mouse-el man!

What did the wizard get when he crossed a rabbit with a rooster?

An ear-ly bird!

What did the wizard get when he crossed a baboon with a tool kit?

A monkey wrench!

What did the wizard get when he crossed fruit with a math book?

Apple pi!

What did the wizard get when he crossed a liar with some Gouda?

Cheater cheese! (cheddar cheese)

What did the wizard get when he crossed a snake and a symphony?

A boa conductor!

What did the blackbird say when it took the dinghy across the moat?

"Crow, crow, crow your boat!"

What did the wizard get when he crossed a squid with a cat?

An octo-puss!

What did the wizard's frog say to the snake?

Hiss me now or lose me forever!

What was the snake's favorite subject in school?

Hiss-story!

What did the wizard's snake use to eat?

Fork-chops!

What did the wizard say when he cast a spell on his snake?

"Abra-da-cobra!"

What did the wizard get when he crossed a lizard with the worker who cut his grass?

A gardener snake!

What did the wizard get when he crossed a vine with a snake?

Poison ivy!

SILLY SPIES

What did the secret agent use to write his autobiography?

Sus-pens! (suspense)

Why did the spy's horse retire?

Because its nerves were shod!

How did the spy feel when he put his hand on the spark plug?

A little shocked!

How did the enemy secret agent like his food?

Scheming hot!

Where did the secret agent catch the dirty crook?

At the scene of the grime!

What do countries call it when they trade agents?

A spy for a spy!

When do villains get read their rights?

When they're in the wrong!

sniff sniff

What did the spy's cat think when it saw the crime scene?

"I smell a rat!"

ಠ‿ಠ

What do spies call the room where all their long meetings are held?

The bored room!

ಠ‿ಠ

What did the secret agent think of the magician spy?

That he was tricky!

ಠ‿ಠ

What do spies call their best basketball squad?

The scheme team!

ಠ‿ಠ

What did the spy do while he made dinner?

He cooked up a plot!

ಠ‿ಠ

What did the secret agent say when he caught the slow spy?

"I've uncovered a vicious plod!" (plot)

ಠ‿ಠ

What did the secret agent say about the suspicious chicken farmer?

"I'll bet he's hatching a plan right now!"

UNDER WHERE?

What do you call underwear that you can't decide whether or not to buy?

Iffy skivvies!

What did they call the monster that ran around in its boxer shorts?

The under-were-wolf!

What did the underwear button say to the hole?

"The eyes have it!"

What do you call a tricky fastener?

A tripper zipper!

How did the man know that his shorts were unhappy?

They got themselves into a real flap!

What do you call long-haired underwear?

Hippies!

How many boxer shorts does it take to make a fruit salad?

Just one pear!

How do you know when your underwear is tired?

When it can't stay up any longer!

Why do you feel so secure in your underwear?

Because you know you're covered!

Why is one sock always missing from the wash?

Because it likes wandering from the laundering!

What do you get when you forget to separate the dark colors from the white boxer shorts?

Blue bottoms!

Knock, knock!
Who's there?
Harlow!
Harlow who?
Harlow do you wear your underpants?

Why did the man think that his loose underwear was like a pizza?

Because he had to pick them up!

Why is the flap on boxer shorts so attentive?

It sits front and center!

How do you know when it's getting late for your underwear?

When time is running shorts!

What do you say when you see someone's underwear hanging out?

"You look like you're waisting away!"

XTREME-LY FUNNY

How did the hard-working skate-boarder get such a flat nose?

He kept it to the grindstone!

Why can't army sergeants be good, relaxed surfers?

Because they're always yelling "Ten-sion!"

Why do skateboarders love to go up hills?

To get away from being grounded!

Why are people dumber at the bottom of a chairlift than they are at the top?

Because the crowds are denser down there!

How did the boarder feel when he got toasted on the hill?

He was a little burned up about it!

How did the blind carpenter make such good skateboards?

He just picked up his tools and saw!

Why didn't the windsurfer believe the story about the piranha attack?

Because it sounded fishy!

What happened when a pile of snow fell from a bough onto the boarder's head?

It knocked him out cold!

Why did the big-air jumper come down with a cold?

Because her tricks were just too sick!

What do you get when you cross a snowboard with an ax?

The splits!

What is the worst part about BMX bikes for mice?

The squeaking!

What is the best thing a motocross racer can take when she feels run-down?

The number of the guy who ran over her!

How are pills and hills different?

One is hard to get down and the other is hard to get up!

What did the boarder get when she cut through the treacherous trees?

A short cut!

What did the boarder's dog get?

Trick ticks!

Wacky Wizardry

What did the wizard's frog say
to the toad?

"So, warts on your mind?"

⭐🌙⭐

What did the wizard get when he crossed
a snowball and a snake?

Frostbite!

⭐☀️⭐

What did the wizard get when he
crossed a heckler with a parrot?

A mockingbird!

⭐🌙⭐

What did the wizard say
to the little bird?

Sparrow a moment?

⭐☀️⭐

What did the wizard get when he
crossed a baseball player
with a chicken?

A fowl ball!

⭐🌙⭐

What did the wizard get when he
combined a duck and a funny book?

Quacker-jokes!

⭐☀️⭐

Where did the wizard get his owl?

The stork market!

⭐🌙⭐

What did the wizard call it when
he pulled a rabbit out of his hat
three times in a row?

A hat trick!

What did the wizard tell the Cyclops who was playing baseball?

"Keep your eye on the ball!"

What did the wizard call the bird with an eye patch?

Polly the Pirate!

What did the witch get when she crossed a school with a circus?

The class clown!

What did the woman say when the wizard told her how much the spell would cost?

"That's a charm and a leg!"

What did the witch get when she crossed a toboggan with some tools?

A sled-hammer!

What did the wizard call his spirit friends from Europe?

Portu-ghosts!

What did the suit of armor say after being left out in the rain?

"I think I'll lie down for a rust!"

What did the suit of armor miss about being worn?

The knight life!

KNOCK, KNOCK!

Knock, knock!
Who's there?
Raymond!
Raymond who?
Raymond me again
what I'm doing here!

Knock, knock!
Who's there?
Madge!
Madge who?
Madge-in my surprise,
you're home!

Knock, knock!
Who's there?
Sammy!
Sammy who?
Sammy directions next time, and
I'll get here faster!

Knock, knock!
Who's there?
Dwight!
Dwight who?
Dwight when I was gonna
tell you, too!

Knock, knock!
Who's there?
Greta!
Greta who?
Greta phone, then I can
stop knocking!

Knock, knock!
Who's there?
Douglas!
Douglas who?
Douglas is broken, they must
have come in at night!

Knock, knock!
Who's there?
Bunny!
Bunny who?
Bunny thing is, I know where the eggs are hidden!

Knock, knock!
Who's there?
Comb!
Comb who?
Comb down and I'll tell you!

Knock, knock!
Who's there?
Eva!
Eva who?
Eva wonder why I always knock?

Knock, knock!
Who's there?
Rabbit!
Rabbit who?
Rabbit around your head like a turban!

Knock, knock!
Who's there?
Ron!
Ron who?
Ron house! Sorry! They all look the same!

Knock, knock!
Who's there?
Roberts!
Roberts who?
Roberts are afraid of alarms!

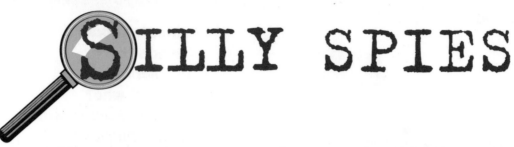SILLY SPIES

Why are spies so good
at playing softball?

Because they're underhanded!

What do you call a female spy?

Miss Chevious!

What do evil agents
call their spy classes?

Wick Ed.!

Where did the spy keep his
important fake beards hidden?

In his must-stash!

What did the gumshoe
think of the spy?

That he was a heel!

Why was the detective suspicious
of the Leaning Tower of Pisa?

*Because there was something
crooked about it!*

Why did the enemy's plan
make the spy feel sad?

Because it was a blue-print!

Why did the spy
hate being underground?

*Because everyone else
thought he was a lowlife!*

What did the enemy spy
call his speech about knots?

His tie-rant! (tyrant)

Why did the spy want a
green thumb?

*So he could plant things
on people!*

What do mean spies drink?

Nas-tea!

How did the spy get her broken-down
stealthmobile home?

She got a tip-tow!

Why didn't the secret agent
like the robot spy?

He just couldn't rust him!

What did the spy say about
the phone conversation
she was tapping?

"This is dial-bolical!"

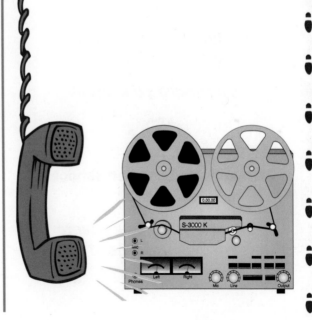

CLASSROOM Crack-ups

What did the student become on his thirteenth birthday?

A teenager!

What is the best way to get by in computer class?

Bit by bit!

Why are math books so hard to get along with?

They have so many problems!

What do you call it when you have to repeat a grade?

Secondary education!

Why are underwater schools so mobile?

Because fish know how to travel in schools!

What did the student say when the teacher accused him of not listening?

"I am listening! I just can't hear you over the snoring!"

What do you call a class in a tree?

High school!

**What kind of snake
is the best at arithmetic?**

The adder!

What kind of table has no legs?

The times table!

**What did the boy say when he
showed up without having his
science experiment done?**

"My homework ate my dog!"

How difficult is it to be impolite?

It's rude-imentary!

**Why did the lowly boy
stay home from school?**

He had no class!

**What do antibiotics and your
school desk have in common?**

*They're both for putting
pencil-in! (penicillin)*

**What kind of plants
do math teachers grow?**

Ones with square roots!

Wacky Wizardry

How did the ghost feel after walking all the way home to the castle?

He was dead on his feet!

What did the wizard call the story that the knight told about his horse?

A pony-tail!

What did the wizard get when he crossed a cola with a bike?

A pop-cycle!

Why did the wizard tell the joke to the ice?

He wanted to see if he could crack it up!

What did the wizard call the knight after his clothes shrank?

Tight in shining armor!

What did the wizard call the zombie's hair?

Mouldy locks!

What did the witch call the movie she was making about the midnight hour?

A dark-umentary!

What did the wizard feed the Italian ghost?

Spook-ghetti!

What did the wizard get when he crossed a banana with a hyena?

Peels (peals) of laughter!

Where did the wizard's daughter find her first boyfriend?

At the Meet Ball!

What did the wizard get when he crossed a scientist with a duck?

A wise-quacker!

Why was the wizard trying to make a legless cow?

To get ground beef!

What did the wizard get when he crossed a frog and a bunny?

A ribbit rabbit!

What did the witch call her popular recipe book?

A best-smeller!

How do witches style their hair?

With scare-spray!

What did the zombie tell the wizard?

"I'm rotten to my friends!"

 XTREME-LY FUNNY

What did the cheap racer say when his doctor gave him his bill?

"I thought you said you were going to treat me!"

How did the boarder feel when he fell into a ski jacket face first?

Just a little down in the mouth!

Why were all the fans at the motocross rally wearing white?

Because they were sitting in the bleachers!

How did the boarder think he could get rich by eating Chinese food?

From the fortune cookies!

What did the rider's friends call him after he crashed on his new yellow board?

Banana splits!

What did the boarder say after being late because her bank was robbed?

"Sorry, I got held up!"

Why was the mathematician such a bad surfer in shark-infested waters?

Because he added four and four and got ate!

What did the sign at the ski slope say?

"Laws of Gravity Strictly Enforced!"

LAWS OF GRAVITY STRICTLY ENFORCED

How did friends calm down the angry sunburned surfer?

They threw water on him so he could let off some steam!

How did the boarder spell "too much air" in just two letters?

X-S!

What do all BMX bikers have in their shoes?

Athlete's feet!

How did the biker feel after she crashed into the pie shop?

A little crusty!

Why do chilled-out boarders hate tennis so much?

They can't stand the racquet!

Why did the skier like the view through his new goggles?

Because he could see from pole to pole!

How did the biker feel when she got a flat in the middle of the race?

A little deflated!

How do big-name skaters stay so cool?

They rely on their fans!

 SILLY SPIES

How did the spy see through the suspect's poncho disguise?

He just knew it was a put-on!

Why do detectives need glasses?

Because they get hint squint!

What did Shakespeare call his spy play?

A View to a Quill!

What happened to the spy with bad vision?

He got a sight-ation! (citation)

What did the spy say when asked how he missed seeing the suspect?

"Eye don't know!"

What did scientists try to develop in the lab to help spies?

Smell-o-vision!

Where do spies rest in the middle of a long pursuit?

Chase lounges! (chaise lounges)

Why were the spies so quiet while they laid their trap?

Because they were waiting with baited (bated) breath!

How did the detective catch his enemy at the pig farm?

With a ham-bush!

What did the spy say about fishing for clues?

"You really have to lure (lower) your standards!"

What do baby spies play with?

Ploy toys!

What do spies call members of their club?

Their peers!

How did the spy know that he was tired from spying all day?

Because he just couldn't get up the stares!

What did the detective think about the dancing lumberjack case?

It was a real jig-saw puzzle!

KNOCK, KNOCK!

Knock, knock!
Who's there?
Avenue!
Avenue who?
Avenue heard this joke before?

Knock, knock!
Who's there?
Santa!
Santa who?
Santa letter telling you I was
coming. Didn't you get it?

SANTA CLAUS
General Delivery
North Pole

Knock, knock!
Who's there?
Moon!
Moon who?
Moon over and let me sit
on the couch!

Knock, knock!
Who's there?
Banana!
Banana who?
Knock, knock!
Who's there?
Banana!
Banana who?
Knock, knock!
Who's there?
Banana!
Banana who?
Knock, knock!
Who's there?
Orange!
Orange who?
Orange ya glad I didn't
say banana?

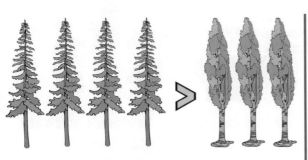

Knock, knock!
Who's there?
Forest!
Forest who?
For-est more than three!

Knock, knock!
Who's there?
Alvin!
Alvin who?
Alvin a nice time on your porch, since you asked!

Knock, knock!
Who's there?
Butcher!
Butcher who?
Butcher money where your mouth is!

Knock, knock!
Who's there?
Tony!
Tony who?
Tony down in there, I'm trying to sleep!

Knock, knock!
Who's there?
Freddy!
Freddy who?
Freddy soon, you're going to find out!

Knock, knock!
Who's there?
Butter!
Butter who?
Butter come inside, it looks like rain!

UNDER WHERE?

What do you call the boxer shorts that you wear at the beginning of the week?

Your Monday undies!

Why did the woman throw out her underwear?

Because they had become moldy oldies!

Where do long underwear go to dance?

The moth ball!

What did one moth say to the other when it saw the long underwear?

"Let's eat!"

What do you call underwear that you change into at noon?

A box-ered lunch!

Why weren't the boxer shorts worried about the stinky rumors they had heard?

They figured it would all come out in the wash!

Why are old boxer shorts worried about getting wet?

Because they really have to wash their figure!

Why were the boxer shorts so proud of themselves?

Because they were snug and smug!

What did the silk underwear say about the cotton boxer shorts?

"Pay them no hind!"

Why didn't the man mind wearing his flannel boxers on the transatlantic flight?

He liked the idea of being snuggled out of the country!

How did the old boxer shorts feel?

Under appreciated!

What do you think about boxer shorts for rabbits?

They're pretty bunny!

Where do boxer shorts for astronauts go?

To underspace!

Knock, knock!
Who's there?
India!
India who?
India morning I always change my underwear!

Why did the man sit on the radiator?

Because he wanted to toast his buns!

What did the boxer shorts say about being ignored?

"Why do you treat me like a bum?"

Wacky Wizardry

Why was the wizard's frog
so full and happy?

*Because it ate everything
that bugged it!*

What did the wizard get when
he crossed a towel with a frog?

A rubbit!

What did the toads in the wizard's swamp
eat when they wanted junk food?

French flies!

Knock, knock!
Who's there?
Ghoul!
Ghoul who?
*Ghoul be sorry if you
don't open up!*

What did the wizard say to
the snake that bit him?

"Fangs a lot!"

Old wizard: "Are you sure that your
spell gave your mother eight legs?"

*Young wizard: "Sure, I'm sure. I
just spider!"*

How did the wizard get his car home
after it broke down?

He toad it!

Why do witches come out only
on Halloween?

*Because they're crazy
for candy!*

What did the wizard get
when he crossed a necklace
with an alarm clock?

A diamond ring!

What was the ogre's favorite dish?

Ghoul-ash!

What did the wizard think
of the scary movie?

He thought it was dreadful!

What kind of movies
do witches like best?

Hag-shun films!

What did the wizard get when he crossed
an elephant with a butterfly?

A mam-moth!

Why do wizards wear pointy hats?

*To keep their sharp
minds warm!*

What did the wizard say when he
cast a sleeping spell on his cat?

*"Why don't you paws
for a moment?"*

What did the toad say when
the princess wouldn't kiss him?

"Warts the matter with you?"

SILLY SPIES

Why did the secret agent think the detective was a fake?

Because he was so unreal-lie-able!

What is another name for spyglasses?

Skeptical spectacles!

What do spies call hiding out at night?

Eve-ation! (evasion)

What did the detective say about the double agent climbing the wall?

"I hope he false down on the job!"

What did the spy call his new hat disguise?

His false hood!

What did the secret agent say about the lying spy?

"He has bad moral fibber!"

What did the spy say about the sneaky bear?

"He's so fur-tive!"

What did the spies call the hidden passage that made the rug stick up?

The trip door!

Why did the computer spy quit?

Because he just couldn't hack it anymore!

Blub
Blub

Why didn't the spy
trust the whale?

*He knew it was a
blubbermouth!*

What did the spies
call their female boss?

Miss Chief! (mischief)

Why didn't the spy
trust the car salesman?

*Because she knew that he was a
trader! (traitor)*

What happened when the spy
got caught on the enemy boat?

She was sent up the river!

What do you call a spy
with a couple of disguises?

Two-faced!

XTREME-LY FUNNY

Why did the BMXer wish that her coach was on the radio?

Because then she could have turned him off!

Why wasn't the boarder worried about the icy patches on the pipe?

He thought that they were skid stuff!

How can a skier jump off a giant mountain and not get hurt?

She can wait until she gets to the bottom!

How did the surfer fix his banana board?

With a monkey wrench!

What time was it when the climbers came across the bear?

Time to run!

Should a surfer ever swim on a full stomach?

No, he should swim on the ocean!

Why did the wimpy racer love to send mail?

She knew that she could at least lick the stamps!

Why did the skier refuse to race against any jungle cats?

Because they were all cheetahs!

What did the boarder think when he saw his picture hanging in a window?

He thought he'd been framed!

Why did the skaters stop hanging out with their slingshot-crazy pal?

He was always shooting his mouth off!

Knock, knock!
Who's there?
Doughnut!
Doughnut who?
Doughnut forget to wear a helmet!

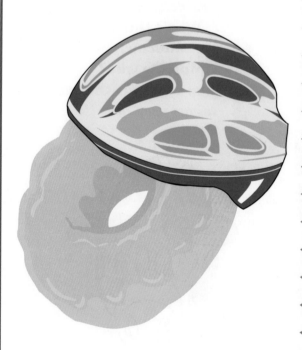

How did the boarder feel when her friend skied right over her?

A little run-down!

What did the climber say to his jacket before he went into a cave?

"Cover me, I'm going in!"

What did the boarder say after nearly cutting herself chopping wood?

"That was almost an ax-ident!"

What do BMXers call police officers assigned to the races?

Cop cycles!

KNOCK, KNOCK!

Knock, knock!
Who's there?
Evans!
Evans who?
Evans to Betsy, you look tired!

Knock, knock!
Who's there?
Berlin!
Berlin who?
Berlin hot out here,
ain't it?

Knock, knock!
Who's there?
Moscow!
Moscow who?
Moscows moo but this one
seems very quiet!

Knock, knock!
Who's there?
Boston!
Boston who?
Boston left me in charge of the
office for the day!

Knock, knock!
Who's there?
Kansas!
Kansas who?
Kansas what tuna
comes in!

Knock, knock!
Who's there?
L.A.!
L.A. who?
L.A. down to take a nap and
I slept right through dinner!

Knock, knock!
Who's there?
Gertie!
Gertie who?
Gertie dishes are no fun!

Knock, knock!
Who's there?
May!
May who?
May my bed for me, would you?

Knock, knock!
Who's there?
Myron!
Myron who?
Myron is clean! Honest!

Knock, knock!
Who's there?
Gladys!
Gladys who?
Gladys finally Friday. I can't take another day of school!

Knock, knock!
Who's there?
Sadie!
Sadie who?
Sadie magic words, and I'll tell you!

Knock, knock!
Who's there?
Ida!
Ida who?
Ida done my homework if my dog hadn't eaten it!

Wacky Wizardry

What did the wizard say about
working with animals?

"It's aard-vark!"

⭐ ☀ ⭐

What did the wizard get when he
crossed a potato with a priest?

A chip-monk!

⭐ 🌙 ⭐

What do wizards do
before they go to bed?

They spell their prayers!

⭐ ☀ ⭐

What did the wizard call the necklace
made out of lettuce?

Salad gold!

⭐ 🌙 ⭐

What did the wizard get when he crossed
a movie star with a monster?

E-lizard-Beth Taylor!

⭐ ☀ ⭐

What did the wizard call
a resting place for birds?

A cemet-airy!

⭐ 🌙 ⭐

What did the wizard call his surly servant?

Stormy waiter!

⭐ ☀ ⭐

How do wizards remember?

They visit Memory Lane!

⭐ 🌙 ⭐

What did the wizard
call the monster that wore a robe?

The Kimono (Komodo) dragon!

Why did the monster's guitar sound better after being in the basement for a long time?

Because it had been tombed! (tuned)

What instrument does a wizard on vacation play?

The Bermuda Triangle!

Where do wizards get their honey?

From spelling bees!

What did the wizard say about the shy witch?

"Oh, she's just bats-full!"

Why did the wizard love to tell jokes to his owl?

Because the owl always gave a hoot!

Which singer do astronomer wizards like best?

Ricky Martian!

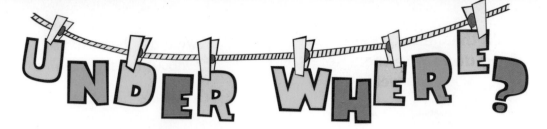

UNDER WHERE?

What did the old man say about his favorite shorts?

"I love my goody two shorts!"

How did the woman feel about her low-rise underwear?

She thought they were pretty hip!

Why did the two legs of the long johns want to stay together?

They were an old couple!

What did the man wear under his suit at the luncheon?

His tea shirt!

What do you call someone who loves to look for underwear?

Short-sighted!

What do you call bright silk briefs?

Shiny tinies!

How did the long johns know that they were going to be shortened?

They saw it coming at the cut-off!

Knock, knock!
Who's there?
Kenya!
Kenya who?
Kenya guess what color my underwear is?

What do you call boxers that are too big?

Roomy bloomers!

How did the captain feel about going down with the ship in his underwear?

He had a shrinking feeling!

What did the underwear call the big, dim-witted man who wore them?

A simple-ton!

Why did the Neanderthal suddenly start wearing underwear?

One day, he just caved!

What kind of shorts did dinosaurs wear?

Bronto boxers!

What do you call shorts held up with ivory?

Waist-boned!

How did the man feel about getting his shorts caught on the door handle?

He was a little hung up about it!

KNOCK, KNOCK!

Knock, knock!
Who's there?
Gorilla!
Gorilla who?
*Gorilla cheese is good
with ketchup!*

Knock, knock!
Who's there?
Eggs!
Eggs who?
Eggs-men are everywhere!

Knock, knock!
Who's there?
Olive!
Olive who?
*Olive the times I've been
to your house and you
still don't recognize me?*

Knock, knock!
Who's there?
Grape!
Grape who?
*Grape game the other day.
You're still the champ!*

Knock, knock!
Who's there?
Stan!
Stan who?
*Stan back, or I'll kick the
door down!*

Knock, knock!
Who's there?
Pizza!
Pizza who?
*Pizza me! I'm as surprised
as you are!*

Knock, knock!
Who's there?
Sonny!
Sonny who?
Sonny side up please!

Knock, knock!
Who's there?
Ooze!
Ooze who?
Ooze the boss around
here, anyway?

Knock, knock!
Who's there?
Shoe!
Shoe who?
Shoe kid, you're bothering me!

Knock, knock!
Who's there?
Julia!
Julia who?
Julia think I'm gonna tell you?

Knock, knock!
Who's there?
Wylie!
Wylie who?
Wylie answers the door, the
bathtub is overflowing!

Knock, knock!
Who's there?
Caesar!
Caesar who?
Caesar before she has time
to fill up her squirt gun!

TEACHER TICKLERS

What did the student say when the teacher reminded her that she'd had detention every day?

"Thank heaven it's Friday!"

What did the student say when the teacher asked why he didn't know any answers?

"If I did, why would I come to class?"

Teacher: "Which month has 28 days?"

Student: "All of 'em!"

Teacher: "I told you to go to the back of the line!"

Student: "I did, but someone was already there!"

Teacher: "Please recite the longest sentence!"

Student: "Twenty-five to life!"

What do you call a teacher who can see with her back turned?

Four-eyes!

What did the students call the teacher who threw surprise tests?

Pops!

Teacher: "Why were things better in 1900 than now?"

Student: "There was less history to learn!"

Teacher: "How can you get so many wrong answers in one day?"

Student: "I start very early!"

What did the student say when the teacher asked where elephants are found?

"You lost an elephant?"

Why should the two chemistry teachers have known better than to date?

They should have seen the science! (signs)

Teacher: "What do you get when you divide 608 by 53?"

Student: "The wrong answer!"

Teacher: "Today we're going to try something different!"

Student: "What's that?"

Teacher: "Learning!"

Teacher: "What proof do you have that the world is round?"

Student: "I didn't say it was, you did! You prove it!"

What is worse than a teacher finding a worm in her apple?

Finding half a worm!

# XTREME-LY FUNNY

How did the cheap boarder work out in the off-season?

By pinching pennies!

What did the boarder's dog have to keep it warm?

A fleas (fleece) coat!

Why did the skier get frostbite on his legs?

Because he couldn't figure out how to get pants on over his skis!

Why do boarders hate doing laundry in the winter?

They're afraid of ring around the colder! (collar)

Why did the boarder buy his dog a fur coat?

Because he didn't want it to be a little bear! (bare)

Why did the skater think that she could glide across the country?

Because she had heard about a coast-to-coast trip!

Knock, knock!
Who's there?
Bailey!
Bailey who?
Bailey me out of the snow!

How did the figure skater know that her skates were tired?

Because their tongues were hanging out!

What did the motocross racer say
after she crossed
the dirty finish?

*Oh, don't give me
that old line!*

What is bright red and
has a trunk?

*A burned surfer heading home
from vacation!*

What did the skateboarder sing
when he saw a cow at the
top of the half-pipe?

*"The hills are alive
with the sound of mooing!"*

How did the surfer feel after
too much coffee?

Really perky!

How do boarders make
their snowpants last?

They put on their jackets first!

How does a boarder make
his bed longer?

He adds his two feet to it!

What did the boarder call the person
who stole his dog?

A spot remover!

Moooo

Wacky Wizardry

What did the wizard
tell the movie star?

**"I think you've got
a fan to see!" (fantasy)**

What did the wizard call the monster
that ate its brother?

A munch-kin!

What did the wizard get when he
crossed a monarch with a snake?

A king cobra!

What did the wizard use
to catch a fish for dinner?

Hali-bait!

What kind of car do
creepy-crawly witches drive?

Beetles!

What did the wizard
call the knight with no home?

The bedless horseman!

What did the wizard call the little
gourds that he had grown?

Pumpkin-bred!

What did the wizard say
to the witty ogre?

**"You've got a troll
sense of humor!"**

What do you call witches
who work in hospitals?

Health scare!

⭐ ☀ ⭐

What did the wizard get when
he crossed a pumpkin with a plant?

A jack-o'-lan-fern!

⭐ 🌙 ⭐

What did the wizard call the cloak
that he had made out of fish?

A cape cod!

⭐ ☀ ⭐

What did the wizard say about
his wife's longest spell?

"She was in a cast for weeks!"

What did the wizard call the twin ghosts?

A-pair-itions!

⭐ ☀ ⭐

What did the wizard make his crazy
friend for dessert?

Upside-down kook!

⭐ 🌙 ⭐

What do you call 12-dozen worms
on a wizard's counter?

Gross!

⭐ ☀ ⭐

When do ghosts graduate?

When they have the fright stuff!

KNOCK, KNOCK!

Knock, knock!
Who's there?
Dill!
Dill who?
Dill we meet again, my sweet!

Knock, knock!
Who's there?
Norma Lee!
Norma Lee who?
Norma Lee I wouldn't come
over this late, but can I
borrow some milk?

Knock, knock!
Who's there?
Canvas!
Canvas who?
Canvas be true?

Knock, knock!
Who's there?
Earl!
Earl who?
Earl gladly tell you if you'd
open up!

Knock, knock!
Who's there?
Bat!
Bat who?
Bat you can't wait to find out!

Knock, knock!
Who's there?
Cherry!
Cherry who?
Cherry this for me, will you? My
back's killing me!

Knock, knock!
Who's there?
Terry!
Terry who?
Terry what, why don't you
lend me a dollar?

Knock, knock!
Who's there?
Epstein!
Epstein who?
Epstein some crazy people,
but you take the cake!

Knock, knock!
Who's there?
Sparrow!
Sparrow who?
Sparrow couple of
quarters, pal?

Knock, knock!
Who's there?
Lark!
Lark who?
Lark I'm going to tell you!

Knock, knock!
Who's there?
Goose!
Goose who?
Goose the doctor,
you look sick!

ILLY SPIES

What did the spy call his
mother's sister?

The auntie hero!

What do you call a spy
who leaves the dinner table early?

A dessert-er!

What did the secret agents
call the spy who was
dim-witted in court?

The evi-dunce!

What do spies say to their children
when they are naughty?

"You are under-grounded!"

What did the secret agent
say about the small magician
who picked pockets?

"He's light of hand!"
(sleight of hand)

What did the detective say when
someone tried to hand him a phone?

"Just the fax, ma'am!"

Why did the ghost spy
love his job?

*Because he just couldn't phantom
(fathom) doing anything else!*

What happened between
the two opposing agents
at the butcher shop?

Ham-to-ham combat!

Why did the spy call the
pat of butter cowardly?

Because it was yellow!

Why was the spy afraid
of telephones?

It was just one of her hang-ups!

How could the spy hear secrets
in the swimming pool?

He knew how to read laps!

Why did the spy have to
take a sick day?

*Because she had
strained her ears!*

Why did the spy have a
cast on his ear?

*Because he had heard
a broken code!*

What did the spy say when he
couldn't find his magician son?

"I lose son!"
(illusion)

XTREME-LY FUNNY

Why did the old-time surfer think he could get his hair cut at sea?

He thought he saw a clipper ship!

What did the biker think about crashing into the wall?

It cracked her up!

What did the young guys call the old surfer who stood around all day?

The dust collector!

How did the boarder feel when he crashed into the baker?

A little crumby!

Why didn't the skater trust her new shoes?

Because she thought they were sneakers!

What did the surfer think of the dentist who fixed his teeth?

He thought she was boring!

What did the skater think of the man who fixed her shoes?

She thought he was a heel!

How did the biker feel about the race after his tire popped?

He felt like he'd blown it!

What did the skaters think of the blue-haired boarder with the big shoes?

They thought he was a clown!

Why did the boarder wear a cabbage on her helmet?

Because she wanted to get a-head!

Why did the skater throw his Airwalks into the competition bowl?

Because he wanted to be a shoe-in!

How did the hang glider feel when he crashed into the garbage?

A little down in the dumps!

What did the diver call the fish doctor?

A brain sturgeon!

How do late-night bike races start?

"On your mark, get set, glow!"

What did the boarder think of the pinecones that the squirrels dropped on him?

He thought they were nuts!

Wacky Wizardry

What did the wizard call the
psychic who kept growing?

Fortune Taller!

What did the wizard call the
monster named Theodore?

Demon-Ted! (demented)

What did the rabbit
say to the sorcerer?

"Wiz up, doc?"

What did the wizard say after his
wife starting throwing dishes?

"Look out! Flying saucers!"

What did the wizard get when he
crossed a planet with a dish?

The World Cup!

What do wizards like
about alphabet soup?

They can spell while they eat!

What did the wizard call the
knight's naughty horse?

A night mare!

What did the wizard's wife say
when he bought her a new cloak?

"Oh, you're so robe-mantic!"

What did the wizard get when he crossed a writing tool with a bird?

A pen-guin!

What did the wizard call the scales he dug up in the backyard?

Buried measure!

What did the wizard call the dog after he had shrunk it?

Spot!

What did the wizard say when his pen exploded?

"I've got that inking feeling again!"

What did the wizard call the jewelry that he gave to his wife?

Married treasure!

How do you know if a wizard is happy?

He's going through a smiling spell!

What do you call a strange hairy wizard?

A beardo!

What did the witch call the wizard with no hair?

Baldy locks!

UNDER WHERE?

What is the best way to get into the whole topic of underwear?

One foot at a time!

What did the man think about his new underwear's waistband?

He thought it was pretty snappy!

What did the man think about his unraveling underwear?

He thought that it had lost the thread somewhere!

Knock, knock!
Who's there?
Abel!
Abel who?
I'm Abel to see your underwear!

What did the sock think about the stuffy underwear?

It thought that it was a little full of itself!

What do you call the most comfy socks around?

Cozy toesies!

Why was the underwear so sad?

Because it was bummed out!

How do you feel when you put on a new pair of boxers?

Short changed!

In what area does your underwear like to hang out?

Near the rear!

What kind of underwear did the big old elephant wear?

Woolly mammoths!

Did it take long for the new underwear styles to become popular?

No, they really cott-on quickly!

Why should suspenders be arrested?

For holding up your shorts!

What did the boxer shorts say to the stockings that were hanging out to dry?

"Oh, don't give me that old line!"

Knock, knock!
Who's there?
Gertie!
Gertie who?
Gertie underwear goes in the hamper!

What did the reader think of the boxer-shorts jokes?

They wore him out!

What do you call a playwright who goes on and on about stockings?

Sockspeare!

Pet Punchlines

Where did the pet bird invest its time?

In the stork market!

Which martial art do ninja budgies practice?

Kung flew!

Why did the parakeet go dutch on dates?

Because he was cheep!

What kind of bird gulps the loudest?

The swallow!

Why are owls so much fun as pets?

Because they're a real hoot to be around!

Why did the little old lady want to get rid of her pet bird?

Because it used fowl language!

When is a dog like a person catching a cold?

When it's a little husky!

Why did the parrot cross the road?

To prove that it wasn't a chicken!

What kind of cat sounds happiest?

A Purrrrsian! (Persian)

What do you say to your pet after it has finished eating its pellets?

"Here's gerbil (your bill), sir. I hope you enjoyed your meal!"

What do you say when you want your pet python to sing with you?

"Let's wrap!" (rap)

What do you call a chicken that makes funny yolks?

A comedi-hen!

Boy: Why don't you believe that I have a pet rat?

Girl: *"Because you're always telling tails!"*

Why don't flying mice make good pets?

Bats me!

KNOCK, KNOCK!

Knock, knock!
Who's there?
Candice!
Candice who?
Candice be any better!

Knock, knock!
Who's there?
Hardy!
Hardy who?
Hardy recognized you without my glasses on!

Knock, knock!
Who's there?
Mice!
Mice who?
Mice to make your acquaintance!

Knock, knock!
Who's there?
Pitcher!
Pitcher who?
Pitcher eye up to the window and see for yourself!

Knock, knock!
Who's there?
Cows go!
Cows go who?
No, they don't! Cows go moo!

Knock, knock!
Who's there?
Ammonia!
Ammonia who?
Ammonia little kid!

Here I am.

Knock, knock!
Who's there?
Beaver!
Beaver who?
Beaver quiet and nobody
will find us!

Knock, knock!
Who's there?
Rat!
Rat who?
Rat seems to be the problem?

Knock, knock!
Who's there?
Howzer!
Howzer who?
Howzer day going?

Knock, knock!
Who's there?
Jason!
Jason who?
Jason you all day is
making me tired!

Knock, knock!
Who's there?
Dogs!
Dogs who?
No, they don't! Owls hoot!

WHOOO!

XTREME-LY FUNNY

What did the diver overhear one fish saying to another?

"One of these days, you'll get caught with your mouth open!"

How did the hungry surfer feel after she'd swallowed some salt water?

It just whet her appetite!

What did the biker say to the horse?

"Hey, why the long face?"

What did the boarders call the longest snowball fight?

The Cold War!

What did the muscle-building biker say when he couldn't get a ring out of his bike?

"Dumb bell!"

What did everyone call the miserly skater who was always wiping out?

Cheapskate!

What do you call the supporters who are first up the hill?

Chair leaders!

How did the diver try to communicate with the big fish?

She thought she would drop it a line!

How did the biker feel after he crashed into the turkey truck?

Pretty stuffed!

Why don't felines surf?

Because they prefer cat-amarans!

What did the boarders call the skeleton who tried to board?

Gutless!

Why are mountain climbers so bad at Christmas?

They just can't resist a peak!

Did you hear about the boarder's fashion crime?

He used a pair of suspenders to hold up his pants!

Why was the poor boarder's dog always chasing its tail?

It was trying to make ends meet!

What did the skater say to the curb?

"I don't want any of your lip!"

What did the boarder's cat hate most about walking home after a rainstorm?

The poodles!

Wacky Wizardry

What did the witch offer guests who stayed at her house?

Broom and board!

What do ghouls call their loudest member?

Their spooksman!

What do witches like to give children for dessert?

Eye scream!

Why was the wizard upset to learn that his spiders were married?

Because he hadn't been invited to the webbing!

What did the spider say to the fly in the wizard's castle?

"Welcome to my Web site!"

Why was the wizard so excited to get his new spiders home?

He wanted to take them out for a spin!

What did the fly call the spider's lair?

A lethal webbin'! (weapon)

What did the witch need when her sewing machine got broken?

A spin doctor!